Cultures of Canada

Arts and Crafts

Edited by
Heather C. Hudak

Weigl

Published by Weigl Educational Publishers Limited
6325 10 Street SE
Calgary, Alberta
T2H 2Z9

www.weigl.com
Copyright ©2010 WEIGL EDUCATIONAL PUBLISHERS LIMITED

Library and Archives Canada Cataloguing in Publication data available upon request.
Fax 403-233-7769 for the attention of the Publishing Records department.

ISBN 978-1-55388-529-0 (hard cover)
ISBN 978-1-55388-534-4 (soft cover)

Printed in the United States of America
1 2 3 4 5 6 7 8 9 0 13 12 11 10 09

Editor: Heather C. Hudak
Design: Terry Paulhus

Every reasonable effort has been made to trace ownership and to obtain permission to reprint copyright material. The publishers would be pleased to have any errors or omissions brought to their attention so that they may be corrected in subsequent printings.

Weigl acknowledges Getty Images as one of its image suppliers for this title.
Alamy: page 22; Canadian Museum of Civilization: pages 11 bottom left, 11 bottom right, 11 top left; Canadian Press: page 10; Decker Colony: pages 15 top right, 15 bottom left; Teena Hughes, http://AbfabDesigns.com: page 19 top left.

All of the Internet URLs given in the book were valid at the time of publication. However, due to the dynamic nature of the Internet, some addresses may have changed, or sites may have ceased to exist since publication. While the author and publisher regret any inconvenience this may cause readers, no responsibility for any such changes can be accepted by either the author or the publisher.

We gratefully acknowledge the financial support of the Government of Canada through the Book Publishing Industry Development Program (BPIDP) for our publishing activities.

Contents

Ukrainian Easter Eggs

Pysanky are Ukrainian Easter eggs. These eggs are hand painted using beeswax and dyes.

Ukrainians use a *kistka* to draw wax designs on an egg. Then, the egg is dipped in dye. The dye sticks to the parts of the egg that are not covered with wax.

LEARN MORE
To learn about pysanky and see pictures, visit http://www.pysankyshowcase.com.

Wooden nesting dolls are common in Ukraine. What other toys can be made from wood?

Embroidered Rushnyky

Gerdan

Matryoshka

Vase

Chinese Paper Cuts

Small scissors and a knife are used to make Chinese paper cuts. Paper cuts have many uses.

Chinese people give paper cuts as gifts. They also use them as decorations and to make clothing patterns. Some paper cuts involve folding, cutting, and pasting many layers of paper.

LEARN MORE
To learn about the history of paper cuts, visit www.chinavoc.com/arts/folk/papercut.htm.

Paper lanterns are part of many Chinese festivals. What crafts do you make for special events?

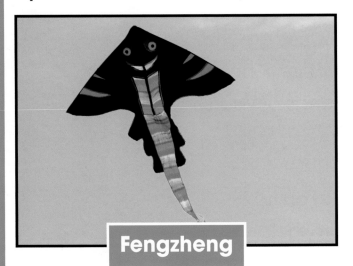

Fengzheng

Ping

Chinese Silk Flower

Lanterns

Sikh Henna Drawings

Sikhs draw detailed pictures on hands and feet. This is called *Mehndi*. Sikhs use ground up henna plant to draw the pictures. They have drawn Mehndi for thousands of years. It often is part of ceremonies.

Sikh brides have Mehndi drawn on their hands and feet the night before their wedding. It is a symbol of the couple's love.

LEARN MORE
To learn how Mehndi is made and used, visit www.puja.com/mehndi.

Sikhs often embroider flowers on their clothing and other items. What other cultures use embroidery to decorate their clothes?

Choora

Phulkari

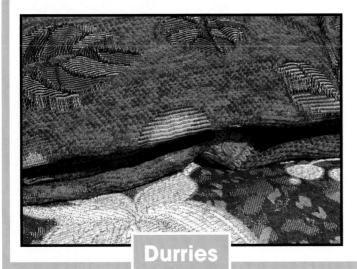

Durries

Henna Patterns

Métis Sashes

Métis make sashes from finger-woven wool. The colours of the sash are red, black, green, blue, and white. Different colour patterns show to which family a Métis person belongs.

Voyageurs worked in the fur trade. They helped move people and goods to different trading posts. Voyageurs often wore the sash. It was tied around the waist to keep a coat closed. The sash was also used as a towel, key holder, and sewing kit.

LEARN MORE
To learn about the history of the Métis sash, visit www.mno.ca/culture/ culture_links/sash.html.

Métis use leather to make many crafts and clothing items. What do you have that is made of leather?

Coat

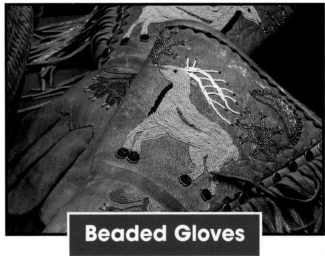

Beaded Gloves

Moccasins

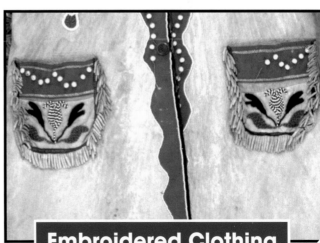

Embroidered Clothing

Jewish Dreidels

A *dreidel* is a four-sided top. Hebrew letters are written on each side of the top. The letters stand for the sentence "A great miracle happened there."

The miracle happened when the Jews won their freedom hundreds of years ago. This is celebrated during Hanukkah.

LEARN MORE

To learn about the dreidels and how to make them, visit www.holidays.net/chanukah/dreidel.html.

Many Jewish arts and crafts are used during prayer services. What items might other cultures use for prayer?

Plates

Wimpel

Shofar

Bimah

Hutterite Carpentry

Some Hutterite men and boys make objects out of wood.

Boys take turns working in the carpenter's shop.

LEARN MORE
To learn about woodworking projects, visit http://biglearning.com/ treasurewood working.htm.

Lebkuchen is a German treat that is similar to gingerbread. When have you seen gingerbread houses in your community?

Schultüten

Lebkuchen House

Embroidery Patterns

Potato Stamp

French Canadian Sugaring

Sugaring is when French Canadians tap maple trees for their sap. They drill a hole in the tree trunk. Then, they place a spout in the hole.

A bucket is hung from the spout to collect the sap. The sap is boiled to make maple sugar. The place where the sap is boiled is called the *Cabane à Sucre*, or "little sugar shack."

LEARN MORE
To learn about the maple tree, tapping, and syrup, visit www.canadianmaplesyrup.com/ maplehistory.html.

Gutta Serti is a special way of painting on silk. What tools do you use when painting pictures?

Gutta Serti

Beaded Flowers

French Horn

Petit Point Patterns

Scottish Knitting

The Scottish knit colourful sweaters, socks, and stockings.

Fair Isle is a type of knitting that uses many colours to make patterns. It is named after a small island north of Scotland.

LEARN MORE
To learn how to knit, visit
http://hubpages.com/hub/Knitting-For-Kids.

Scottish people blow into bagpipes to make music. What other instruments need air to make sound?

Kilt

Doll

Sporran

Bagpipes

Filipino Basket Weaving

Filipinos weave bamboo strips to make baskets. The baskets are known for their strength and beauty.

Some skilled weavers can make baskets in just a few minutes.

LEARN MORE
To learn how to weave a basket, visit www.basketweaving101.net.

Bamboo is used to make many items in the Philippines. What other arts and crafts can be made using bamboo?

Shell Necklace

Parols

Straw Hats

Bamboo Mats

Glossary

bimah: a raised platform with a reading desk from which the Torah is read

choora: bangles worn by Indian brides

durries: hand-knotted mats or bedding

fengzheng: a kite

gerdan: a beaded necklace

gutta serti: the art of painting on silk

henna: a flowering plant that can be ground in hot water to make a dye

kilt: a knee-length skirt that has a plaid pattern

lebkuchen: baked product similar to gingerbread

matryoshka: wooden dolls that have smaller dolls inside

moccasins: shoes made from soft leather that do not have a heel

parols: star-shaped Christmas lanterns that are made from bamboo or paper

petit point: a type of embroidery

phulkari: flower embroidery

ping: a Chinese vase

rushnyky: a homemade cloth with embroidery on each end that is used for special occasions

schultüten: cardboard cones that can be filled with toys, sweets, or school supplies

shofar: a musical horn

sporran: a leather or fur pouch that hangs at the front of a kilt

wimpel: long strip of cloth that is used to wrap around the Torah scroll when it is not in use

Index